How to Sell on eBay
Get Started Making Money on eBay and Create a
Second Income from Home

Richard G Lowe, Jr

How to Sell on eBay
Get Started Making Money on eBay and Create a Second Income from Home

Earn Money from Your Home Series #1

Published by The Writing King
www.thewritingking.com

How to Sell on eBay ™

ASIN: B01H9BSCAW
ISBN: 978-1-943517-36-7 (Paperback)
ISBN: 978-1-943517-35-0 (eBook)

Library of Congress Control Number: 2016910287

For more information see:
www.thewritingking.com

Table of Contents

Introduction

In six months, I made $7,500 by selling merchandise on EBay; even better, I already owned everything I sold. I made this extra income by clearing out my closets, dressers, desk drawers, bookshelves, and so forth, listing products that I had purchased years before and no longer needed or wanted.

All of these things were taking up valuable space in my home, and, on the whole, they were still worth quite a bit of money. Even though I no longer needed or wanted all of this clutter, I felt there would be quite a few people out there who find my undesired belongings valuable.

The purpose of this book is to pass along the lessons that I learned while selling my stuff on EBay and, at the same time, making a little bit of extra income. This money helped pay off a few credit cards, and made the budget a little less tight. The companion book to this volume, Make Money by Decluttering Your Home, goes into detail about how to convert your clutter into cash. A third volume, Make Money Using the Internet to Build a Second Income and Create your Own Business, gives you other ways to increase your income while working from home.

Once I had taken the leap into EBay, I decided to expand my efforts by finding merchants that would sell me merchandise to resell. These included local flea markets, swap meets, sales at department stores, and so forth. Even specials on web sites such as Amazon can serve as sources for merchandise to resell on EBay at a good price and reasonable profit.

How I Got Started on EBay

Over the years, I've dabbled with selling on various online stores, including EBay, usually just an item now and then. I had no idea what I was doing, and EBay, in particular, appeared to be complicated and difficult to confront. Nonetheless, everything I listed sold quickly for a reasonable price. Most of the other online stores were disappointments, resulting in few sales and leading to a lot of wasted effort.

I also used EBay to make a few purchases now and again and was happy to discover that I could find just about anything that I wanted. I bought marble collections, rocks, crystals, used books, movies and an old Super Nintendo console complete with a couple of games and cheater module. It was easier than hunting around for what I wanted at thrift stores, hobby shops, and other places all around town.

A few years ago, I decided it was time to do a purge of my library of paperback and hardcover books. I realized that I was never going to read them all. I began by listing them on Amazon since that seemed to be the right place to sell books. In about four months I sold roughly 200 volumes and made between $600 and $700, after fees and shipping. Not a lot of money, to be sure, but much better than throwing the books out or leaving a big box of them at the library.

Late in 2015, I noticed that I had two closets, a chest of drawers, and several bookshelves filled with still more books, movies, board games, video games, and other collections that I had not even looked at in years and some cases decades.

Time to do another purge!

I went back to the familiar territory of Amazon and found that things were a little bit different than they had been. The site hadn't changed that much, but there seemed to be quite a few more sellers than there had been in the past.

The hundred or so books that I listed sold much slower than they had in the past. With a little research, I discovered the competition was extraordinarily high, and buyers seem to be favoring extremely low-priced books – sometimes as low as a penny plus shipping. In my mind, that's a ridiculous rate; it's impossible to make any decent money with a profit margin that low.

There were new fees, and the old charges had increased. I tried my hand at their FBA program – sending products to Amazon and letting them do the shipping – and that was a disaster. The costs were high, and sales were weak, so I wound up losing money on virtually everything. Eventually, I had them ship everything back and abandoned Amazon as a seller.

I still wanted to do a purge but didn't relish the idea of throwing everything away. I felt there was the opportunity to make some decent money if I could find the right place to sell.

In frustration, I took a closer look at EBay. I listed a few items, and to my surprise, they sold in a matter of days. In that first organized effort, I made a couple of hundred dollars from selling about a dozen things.

After a bit more experimentation, I concluded that EBay would work just fine for my home decluttering project.

Since I'd already made some purchases, I began selling with a high feedback score. I'd learned the value of this score while shopping; sellers with a lower value had a lot of negative comments, indicating they made mistakes and delivered poor customer service.

Beginning with my DVD collection, I jumped back into EBay. Within three months, I had brought in several thousand dollars without a lot of effort. Most of this stuff was in pretty good shape – some still in shrink-wrap – and virtually all of it sold quickly at decent prices.

All of my neighbors have at least a closets or two filled with old games, movies, kid's toys, collectible items, books, clothes, and Lord knows what else. Some of them even rent space to fill with even more old, unused or unneeded stuff.

Think of everything that you own and don't use as wasted money.

Worse yet, you're paying hard earned dollars for the space to store all that stuff, which is even more apparent if you're renting a storage unit. Several families in my neighborhood have entire rooms of their homes filled with old stuff that they will never use again but cannot bear to throw away.

Once you sell off much of your clutter, you can go one step further by finding local sources for merchandise that you can resell on EBay. Thrift stores, sales at big-box stores, flea markets, swap meets, and hundreds of other locations are excellent places to find items that other people want to buy.

Of course, you have to be careful, especially if you are a collector or a bit of a hoarder, that you don't use this as an opportunity to purchase more junk. You have to make a commitment to sell everything you buy within a certain amount of time; this means you need to be aware of what sells quickly and avoid those items that sell slowly if at all.

Let's Get Started

My mission with this book is to help people make a little extra money by taking advantage of the excellent opportunities presented by EBay. There are plenty of other classified and auction sites on the web — many of the concepts discussed herein will apply to them as well — but EBay is by far and away the king.

If you put more than a little bit of effort into the process, you might even find yourself making a good second income, enough to help you get ahead, pay off a few bills, or go on a nice vacation.

This book is not intended to be a step-by-step tutorial on the EBay system. You can use the EBay help files to learn the details of exactly how to perform any task within their application.

The purpose of this book is to explain how you can use EBay to supplement your income, make a few extra dollars, and help you avert some of the pitfalls and mistakes.

I have intentionally avoided going into the more advanced selling techniques, although I do touch on a few such as drop shipping. My primary purpose is to get you started so you can make some extra money to help with your expenses.

The more advanced techniques can be learned later, and EBay has plenty of tutorials and reference materials to help you along. To help even more, I will be writing a book about advanced EBay selling techniques, with an anticipated publication date in the summer of 2016.

The folks at EBay have created an incredible platform that enables anyone to buy and sell virtually anything from anyone else on the planet. If you have an Internet connection and a computer, it's easy for you to use this machine to your advantage.

Read this book thoroughly to make sure that you understand the ins and outs of EBay. Use the site, if you haven't already, and make a few purchases, so you get a feel for how it works. Be sure to pay for your purchases quickly to build up your feedback score.

Once you're confident that you understand how to use EBay by making purchases and exploring, place a few items up for sale. Make sure these are easy to ship —

not too bulky, not fragile, and not odd shapes; Of course, you can sell this kind of thing on EBay, but doing so introduces additional challenges in shipping, and it's best to confront them after you get a little experience.

Once your confidence is up, and you understand the system, jump right in by creating more listings and selling more products. As I said earlier, a great place to start is with your clutter – things that you own that you probably will never use or even look at again. You can do this for no cost and virtually no risk.

As you become more successful at selling, look around your local area to find places where you can purchase things to resell. If you want to go to the next level after that, you need to find wholesalers and drop shippers and do all of the things necessary to create a real business.

It's a great adventure, and it's a relatively easy way to bring in some extra money. Give it a shot and you may earn the extra income you've needed and perhaps get a little ahead of those bills and expenses.

What this Book is Not

This book is intended to teach you the basics of selling on EBay, but I've intentionally not gone into detail on the mechanics. The documentation provided by EBay is excellent and there are many good articles available by searching on your favorite search engine.

My goal is to help people make some extra money quickly and easily by selling things the already own, and prompt them on how to make the jump into even more money by reselling products they purchase locally and online.

If you read this book and follow the guidelines, you should find yourself set up with a nice monthly income. You can then increase that income as much as you want, depending upon how much work you put into the process.

Thus, this book is intended as a starting point to give you an introduction and outline some of the tactics that have been proven to work effectively.

Buying on EBay

Practice By Being an EBay Customer

Before you begin selling, spend some time exploring EBay thoroughly, preferably by making purchases. It's best to understand the process from the purchasing point-of-view before you start working with it as a seller. That way you'll have a better understanding of how the whole process works so you can use it more to your advantage.

Think of a few things you'd like to purchase. They shouldn't be expensive. Begin by making a list of a dozen items in different categories – that's important – that you need or want to add to your collection.

For example, one of the things that I collect is cigar boxes filled with marbles. You can find these on EBay for between $20 and $40. I also collect round stones, crystals, and Disneyland pins, all available for a relatively small cost.

Once you have a list, work through the system as a buyer and learn what you can.

Understand Categories

Learn how categories work. Understand that each item listed on EBay is in at least one category – and can be in two if the seller pays extra.

The highest level categories begin broadly, as with "Toys & Hobbies", and work down to the most precise, "glass marbles, 1950-59." For example, suppose you are looking for marbles. You'd start from a category of *Toys & Hobbies*, followed by *Marbles*, which would then be split up into date ranges which divide further into different types of marbles – vintage, handmade and machine marbles. These categories and subcategories make it easy for a shopper to drill down from the general to the specific to find what they need.

If you look at the left side of the EBay screen, you'll see several check boxes which allow you to pick even more specific criteria such as brand names, condition, style, price range and so forth.

All of this makes it easy for a savvy shopper to find what they want to purchase.

Alternately, shoppers can type in some text in the search box and completely ignore categories and other criteria. If you know what you are looking for, this method can be useful. For example, if I want to find a movie, I can type the title directly into the search bar and pull up everything that matches.

All of these different things are important for you to understand as a seller because these are all part of the listing that you create for your merchandise. You define the category for your product, and all of the other criteria such as manufacturer, age grouping and so forth, to make it easier for your purchasers to find what they want.

Types of Selling

Make sure you understand the difference between selling for a *fixed price* and using an *auction*. A fixed price item goes for an exact price, although the seller can allow buyers to request a lower one. Auctions, on the other hand, work on a bid system. Thus, one person places a bid to purchase an item, and another person makes a higher offer, and then another a little bit more. When the time is up, the person who offered the most money gets the purchase. The seller can check the *buy it now* checkbox to allow purchasers to skip all of that and just buy the product at a specified price.

Choosing the right kind of format, fixed-price or auction, can mean higher profits for you. Sometimes selecting the wrong one results in no sale or a lower selling price than warranted. Thus, it's a good idea to understand these thoroughly. As you gain experience, you'll get an understanding of which items work well in auctions and which as fixed-price.

Shipping and Checkout

Spend some time reviewing the checkout process – known as the shopping cart. It's vital that you understand how this works because all of your customers will be using it to make their purchases.

Virtually everything on EBay is shipped, although there is a rarely used option for local pick-up only. As you explore EBay as a buyer, note the different kinds of shipping options available on various products. Make sure you understand what all of these mean.

Examine a few products before you make any purchases. Look at the descriptions, titles, characteristics, and everything else about those listings. As a buyer, what do you want to know? If you're purchasing new clothes, do you need to know the size? The manufacturer? The material? Those are all things that you must enter when you create similar listings.

On each item, examine the description. Does it tell you what you need to know about it? Or do you get frustrated because it's just a short, barely understandable sentence? Note what works for you and what doesn't. This information will help you as you write descriptions for your products.

As you can see, by purchasing a few items and exploring EBay, you will learn to search by category, what you need to write in descriptions, become familiar with the checkout process and so on. Doing this will help you determine what is necessary and desirable for you to implement when you start to sell.

Feedback

A primary reason for making one or two dozen purchases before you attempt to sell is to build up your reputation, known as feedback, on EBay.

EBay works very hard to get every buyer and seller to leave a feedback rating and comment for each purchase. This feedback helps everyone by showing in a single glance if a seller or buyer can be trusted.

A seller with a good feedback score will get far more sales than one with a poor value.

Additionally, EBay rewards sellers who have high feedback scores by giving them discounts and other perks, and those whose scores are low get penalized.

The same feedback number applies to both purchases and sales.

Maintaining a good feedback store as a buyer is pretty simple. Just pay your invoices quickly, and don't make unreasonable demands on your sellers.

Once you've made a few purchases, and built up your feedback score a bit, it's time to dip your feet into the pool and sell a few things on EBay.

Selling on EBay

Start Small and Easy

Now that you've familiarized yourself with how EBay works for buyers, and you understand how to use categories, listings, and other features, you are ready to begin selling.

A good place to start is to continue to focus on building up your feedback score. Do this by selling some small, inexpensive products, such as collectible stamps, Disneyland pins, and other similar, relatively inexpensive items.

I owned six 2012 Rose Parade pins featuring Trader Joe's. I listed them on EBay for $3.95 each plus postage as a single listing with a quantity of six. They sold out within a matter of a few days, and each buyer entered a feedback rating, which resulted in six positive ratings and good comments for a single, easy to ship product.

Another reason to do this is to get familiar with all of the tools available for selling, shipping, and dealing with your customers. While a buyer can give you a negative feedback score for any size purchase, I've found they are reluctant to do so for small value items.

Creating Your Listings

You can use an existing listing as a starting point to create a new one. To do to do this, search for your merchandise on EBay. When you find it, you will see a button just below the picture labeled *Sell now*. Click that to sell the same product, which fills in some of the attributes for you and saves you a bit of time. Be careful to review your listing to ensure the information is correct.

You can also enter the information about your product from scratch. EBay has a massive database of goods, so most likely it will recommend an appropriate category, which you can accept, or you can choose your own.

Regardless of how you create your listing, EBay will request that you enter the rest of the information about your product. Some of the fields are mandatory, such as the title, a short description, and a picture, and others are optional.

The chapter listing your products describes in detail how to create a product listing. Photos are especially important – See photos for more information – and the quality can mean the difference between making a sale or not.

Always provide honest information. At first glance, you might surmise that you can sell products quickly by exaggerating benefits or quality, or by not including flaws. However, doing so will result in a higher rate of returns and refunds — regardless of whether you state you except refunds are not — and possibly fraud reports to EBay.

Communicate Often

It's a good idea to communicate often with your customers. EBay will automatically send emails throughout the process. You'll receive an email when a product has sold, and the buyer will receive one confirming shipment. You can send more messages as needed to keep your customer informed and to get additional information. More detail about communicating with your clients is in the section Get them back with Good Customer Service.

Sell Quality Products

It is true that EBay is a fantastic place to sell products and an excellent way to help you declutter your home, and clean out closets or storage units of your unused stuff. However, keep in mind that you shouldn't be selling junk. Your merchandise should be of high quality. Be sure to describe flaws or quality issues in your item description.

Costs and Shipping

Become knowledgeable about all of your costs, including EBay fees, shipping charges, and supplies. (Shipping is further described in the chapter titled Shipping.)

For low-profit items, the costs of shipping can reduce or even eliminate your profit. In some cases, if you're not careful, you may find yourself taking a loss, which defeats the purpose of selling on EBay.

At the beginning of each month, EBay gives you some free listings, which is sufficient to cover the listing fees for the vast majority of EBay sellers. If you exceed that number of listings, EBay will charge you a small amount each time you list an item.

If the item doesn't sell and gets relisted, you'll be charged that fee again. For example, if the cost is thirty cents per listing, and your product gets relisted ten times, you'll be charged three dollars.

EBay will also charge you a percentage of your sale as a commission.

You can choose to pay for shipping yourself — out of your profits — or charge the customer for the cost.

It's easy to overlook the price of envelopes and boxes, packing materials, tape, staples, and so forth. If you buy these from your local office store, you could find yourself paying a very high premium to ship your products.

If you're going to be selling for any length of time, it's best to go to a site like Amazon and find envelopes, boxes and packing materials that you can purchase in bulk. See Equipment and Supplies for more information. For a list visit:

https://www.thewritingking.com/ebay-equipment-supplies/

Keep track of all of these costs because they are business expenses that you can use to reduce your taxes at the end of the year. They get listed as expenses on Schedule C if you itemize your deductions. See your accountant and tax advisor for more information.

Equipment and Supplies

Equipment

One of the beautiful things about selling on EBay is you don't need to purchase much equipment. In fact, when you're first starting out, you don't need anything at all, but as your sales increase you'll find a few things that will make life simpler and save you money.

For an up-to-date list, see

https://www.thewritingking.com/ebay-equipment-supplies/

Postal scale — When I first started selling on EBay, I estimated the weight of each package by picking it up. After a few months of doing that, I asked one of the postal employees to weigh a box and found that I overestimated by 2 pounds, which meant I was paying as much as a dollar extra for shipping.

Purchasing a small postal scale on *Amazon* will cost around forty dollars. But it could save you far more than that in the medium to long run.

Barcode reader — A cheap USB barcode reader (you can find a good one on *Amazon* for less than $20) can save you a lot of time. I purchased one of these handy devices and used it to scan the ISBN numbers on the back of the DVD cases of movies, requiring just a quick point-and-click instead of entering the code or title manually.

Digital camera — You can use the camera on your cell phone to take photos of your merchandise. However, a digital camera, with a tripod, will improve your pictures and your chances of getting sales. You don't need to spend a lot of money. A good, inexpensive one will run you between $100 and $200. Don't forget to purchase a high-capacity SD card (or whatever kind of card your camera uses) and a tripod. You can use a small, table-top version if the items you are photographing are small.

If your computer doesn't accept SD cards, you may need to buy a multi-card reader which plugs into your USB port. These usually run around twenty dollars.

A photo lighting kit with lights — Lighting is essential for taking good pictures. A desktop-light kit, which will run about $40 on *Amazon*, contains two small lights mounted on tripods which you can position, eliminating the need to use your flash to take photos.

Photography light tent — A small light tent, which is a box open in the front and top, along with some colored backgrounds will let you take photos of your merchandise without the distracting background clutter.

Supplies

If you are only selling a few things on EBay, then you don't need to spend much time thinking about supplies. A few boxes or padded envelopes and some packing tape may be all you need to get rid of those old toys now that the kids have grown up, or to clean out those games that have been sitting the closet for decades.

On the other hand, the cost of shipping supplies can quickly eat away at your profits. For example, I began by selling off my DVD collection, and the best way to ship DVDs is with small padded envelopes. I found that I could purchase these from the local "discount" office supply store, but they were expensive. After some searching, I discovered good quality shipping envelopes listed on *Amazon* at a much lower cost.

Envelopes — Envelopes of all sizes can be useful for shipping product that lies flat. Stamps, baseball cards, magazines and similar merchandise may not require padded envelopes. It's best to find a source that sells them in *bulk*, which can save quite a bit of money.

Padded envelopes — DVDs, CDs, and other small items require padded envelopes. Purchasing them at your local office store is expensive, especially if you only buy one or two. You can get them in bulk from *Amazon* or EBay for a lot less money.

Boxes — Boxes are surprisingly costly, and they can quickly eat into your profits. You can save money by reusing boxes, or you can find inexpensive boxes in bulk on *Amazon* or EBay.

Packing materials — Peanuts (those annoying Styrofoam pieces) and other supplies cushion your products, which helps them survive a trip through the mail without damage. These can be very expensive if not bought in bulk.

You can be creative when you choose packing materials. Peanuts, bags of air, crumpled up newspapers, and pieces of cardboard will do the job just fine.

Make sure you weigh your shipping container after you've included all of the packing materials.

Shipping tape — Shipping tape is not very expensive, but you will probably go through a lot of it. Shop around both *online* and locally to find an inexpensive source to purchase tape that's durable enough for the job. There is no need to spend a lot of money on shipping tape. The cheapest brand will do just fine.

When to use EBay

Shipping Caveats

EBay is the perfect place to sell many different kinds of merchandise. For products such as DVDs, books, movies, knick knacks, prints, video games, and so forth, there is not a better online store on the entire web.

As I've said before, large items, regardless of whether they are heavy or not, can be difficult to ship. In these instances, websites such as Craigslist, which specify local pickup, may be better suited.

Bulky items present the same difficulties. A friend of mine tried to sell some large barstools, television sets, and similar products that weighed between 70 and 150 pounds each. These required high shipping costs and careful packing. Even so, in over half the cases the items arrived damaged and unusable, and he had to issue refunds to the customers.

When I first started out, I listed a large framed print, with glass. I sold it in an EBay auction, and the final bid was for $60. I didn't think much about the shipping and charged about $10.

Believe it or not, it's difficult to ship a 24x36 framed, glass covered print. In fact, by the time I was done purchasing the special box, padding, tape, postage and everything else, I wound up losing $10 on the deal. Not only did I not make any money, but it took a couple of hours to get the thing ready to ship. These days, when I want to send art in frames with glass, I pay for the packing service at the local UPS store. It is well worth the cost due to the savings in time.

Quality and Listings

We've gone over much of the information in this section before, but it bears repeating. Product quality and thorough descriptions are vital to maintaining high sales and excellent feedback.

EBay is not the same as your local swap meet or flea market. Items listed on EBay are expected to be in good shape, and of at least reasonable quality. You can sell rusty tools at the swap meet, but unless they are antiques EBay is probably not the right venue for them.

Collectible or rare merchandise sells well on EBay. I've sold first edition books for hundreds or even a thousand dollars, an original Dungeons & Dragons game for $400, and animation cells for $600. These items had been sitting on a shelf for over forty years, and so looked a little bit worn. Nonetheless, they sold quite well on EBay.

Earlier in this book, I recommended beginning your EBay adventures by decluttering or purging things that you already own. It is not unusual for a home to have one or more closets stacked high with old games, costume jewelry, clothes, records, laser disks, old equipment, older model computers, books, magazines, stamps, camping supplies and so forth.

A good percentage of these objects are very suitable for selling through EBay. You've already purchased them, so there's no monetary outlay for things to sell. All you need to do is identify your stuff, photograph each item, create the listings, and wait for buyers.

For example, I've been slowly selling off the contents of a closet which contains about a hundred plastic models, a couple of dozen wooden model boats, camping gear, a bubblegum machine, a couple of old computers (which still work), several cameras, and a few other things. These items will net me about $3,000 on EBay. Not bad for a closet full of junk that I'll never use again.

I've got another cabinet which contains about forty costumes, including a Santa outfit, a dozen Renaissance costumes, a vampire costume, a couple of fencing swords, and numerous props and other unusual items that I'll never use again. All of is perfect to sell on EBay.

A friend of mine has a closet full of games, and another one filled from floor to ceiling with old toys. His children are long gone from the house, having grown up and moved out, leaving him with a huge pile of belongings that he will never use again. All of these things could all be sold on EBay and probably bring in one or two thousand dollars.

Item Condition

In some cases, poor quality items sell very well. For example, I wanted to purchase an older game called

Operation with a particular picture on the cover — a drawing of the Doctor smoking a cigarette. This game is no longer sold with that cover because it is considered politically incorrect. I found several of them on EBay in various conditions: one with a big tear in the box, another missing several pieces, one missing the light for the nose, and another missing the tweezers. All of these games sold quickly; I kept looking and finally found one in perfect condition.

In another instance, I owned an older computer which was no longer operational. I was about to throw it away (at the recycler of course) when on a whim I checked it out on EBay and found that some of the parts were selling for pretty good money. I was able to sell the disk drives, cooling fans, memory, video cards, Ethernet card and other devices separately for few hundred dollars. Pretty decent money for a computer that I was going to throw out. (Be sure to use a disk eraser application before you sell or throw away disk drives – see my book Safe Computing is Like Safe Sex for tips on safely disposing of old equipment.)

To determine if an item is salable on EBay, use EBay's search capability. Enter the description of the merchandise — or better yet the model number, ISBN code, or other identifying value — and you will more than likely find that object already listed. Examine some of those listings to get an idea the condition of the merchandise, the price, and the cost of shipping. At that point, you can make an informed decision about whether or not you want to sell your item.

Getting Paid

Only accept payment through EBay. Receiving payment (and then canceling the listing) by any other means is considered a transgression of EBay's terms and conditions and could result in the termination of your account.

EBay provides some protections for both buyers and sellers. The company serves as a broker between the two parties, effectively guaranteeing the seller receives payment before shipping the product. Even if EBay doesn't catch you accepting money outside of their system, you forgo all of their protections if you don't follow their payment rules.

The safest means to receive payment is to connect your PayPal account to EBay. After you've established yourself as a responsible seller, EBay will immediately transfer the funds for each sale directly into your PayPal account.

By doing this, you don't need to worry about how buyers pay for the products. They can use a credit card, debit card, direct payment from their checking account, or any number of other methods, and it's completely irrelevant to you. EBay and PayPal handle all of that behind-the-scenes.

You pay a small fee for that convenience, but in my opinion, the ease of use and security of PayPal far outweigh any inconveniences.

Rarely, you'll run into a buyer who can't or won't pay for their product. EBay recommends you wait for payment before shipping. If you follow this policy and use PayPal, you will never ship product without getting paid.

However, sometimes buyers don't pay quickly. In this case, the best policy is to send them a message using EBay's messaging facility reminding them to pay their invoice, or send them an invoice itemizing their purchases. When a buyer hasn't paid in five days, my procedure is to send them a message telling them payment is due.

If you can't resolve it with the buyer, you can open a case with EBay, who will take over the problem from that point. They will communicate with the customer asking for payment, and if the buyer still doesn't pay, will let you close the case and terminate the sale. The buyer will not be able to give you negative feedback if you use this procedure. (You can automate this process in your EBay settings.)

Every once in a while, before I ship, I'll get a message from a buyer requesting extra time to pay. Sometimes they want to wait until payday, or a check has cleared or something like that. In every case, I was happy to hold on, since they were kind enough to send a message, and they've always followed through with their promise. When you get one of these messages, it's important to reply to let them know whether or not you'll accept their request.

Occasionally, you'll run into scammers who attempt to con you into shipping product without paying. These scammers use what's called social engineering — a con game — to convince you to move outside of the safe boundaries provided by EBay and PayPal. They seem very sincere, persuasive, smooth talking, and friendly. To prevent yourself from being scammed, always follow the EBay rules for accepting payment and shipping. The moment you step outside of the rules, you set yourself up for being scammed. Worse yet, in these cases, EBay will not help you, and you will lose your money and possibly your EBay account.

One of the common scams is for a buyer out of the country to offer to write you a check for your merchandise. They hope that you ship the product before the check clears. This scam works because the bank places a hold of a week or more on the funds. The check will bounce, and if you ship the items before it clears, then you'll never receive payment.

In another case, a buyer might request a local pickup for your product, saying, "Let's save on the EBay fees and shipping by meeting each other a local supermarket. You cancel the listing and I'll pay in cash."

Not only does this violate EBay policy, which can result in the suspension of your account, but it puts you in danger of getting mugged, robbed or worse.

I have found that the combination of EBay and PayPal works extraordinarily well. Sell the product; the buyer pays for it; money winds up in the PayPal account; EBay sends a message when it's okay to ship, and finally package up the product and deliver it to the post office.

Finding Stuff to Sell

Once you have some success selling your clutter, if that's where you decided to start your EBay career, you may want to expand your operations. From my experience, the extra money coming from EBay has turned out to be very useful. I wanted to keep the money coming, so I began exploring other ways to keep my store stocked.

There are an unbelievable number of places where you can get merchandise to sell in your EBay store.

As I've said numerous times already, a good place to start is with your belongings. Go through it all, again and again, selling off the things that you don't need, don't use or don't want. Any stuff that you have stashed in storage units or closets, in boxes under the bed, in the garage, in unused bedrooms, and so forth should be carefully examined, and mercilessly purged and sold on EBay.

It's amazing how much better you'll feel once you eliminated some of the material things that don't contribute towards the quality of your life. These objects weigh you down, keep you in one place, and even worse, they don't give you any value in return.

Not to mention that you could make a pretty penny selling it all off.

Once you've found yourself exhausting your belongings, it's time to expand your horizons, assuming that you want to continue making income from EBay.

One of the reasons to begin with your belongings to give you a chance to find out what sells well and what doesn't, without investing much money in the process. For example, I've found that TV series sell very quickly on EBay for good prices. Plastic and wooden models of all types sell very well, and role-playing games such as Dungeons & Dragons command a good price.

However, music CDs don't seem to sell as fast, and books, regardless of subject, didn't go anywhere.

Selling your stuff also favors your knowledge and strengths. Since presumably you, or members of your family, purchased most of your belongings, you probably know about them and understand their value.

Keep the knowledge you've gained from this experience in your mind as you search for things to sell. It's a good idea, at least at first, to stick with what you know and have experienced. It's very easy to fall into the trap of purchasing something that appears inexpensive believing that it will sell, and then finding yourself with boxes of junk that you have to throw away later.

For example, if you collect stamps, you can use EBay to sell off areas of your collection that no longer interest you. You understand philately (stamp collecting) because you've been purchasing them for a long time, and you have some idea of their value and the terminology related to the subject. This information will help you when buying stamps with the intention of selling them on EBay.

A friend of mine collected dolls and had more than a hundred of them. Her collection became less important to her after her childhood. They gathered dust on her shelves, and she eventually moved them into boxes and put them in storage. She felt she had to keep them – after all, she'd paid too much money to throw them out or give them away.

Once she made the jump into EBay, she found that her dolls sold well and commanded good prices. She got used to receiving an extra thousand dollars a month of income, and as she ran out of dolls to sell she began searching for places where she could purchase them to resell on EBay.

Since she understood dolls very well, she was quite successful at purchasing merchandise that would resell quickly for good prices.

The key is to avoid tying up your money in products that don't sell, or that sell slowly. Remember that merchandise that is sitting on a shelf or in boxes – this is called inventory – ties up money. Look for products that sell fast and which command good prices to avoid maintaining large inventories (*drop shipping* is a good way to get around the inventory problem.)

Your local swap meets and flea markets are great places to start your search for saleable products. A friend of mine, Ted, visits the local swap meet every weekend to find things that he can resell. He understands tools, having been a mechanic most of his life, so that's the focus of his search for products. Usually, he returns from his expeditions with a box of hammers, pliers, and dozens of other tools which he quickly loads up to EBay and sells.

Another friend, Evangelina, sometimes visits the local thrift stores, looking for things to resell. She told me about a black cross that she found and purchased for $35. She resold it on EBay for over $450. She understands this type of product and knows what to look for in the thrift stores. She doesn't buy much, but what she purchases sells quickly and with a good profit.

Estate sales are another excellent source of merchandise. These types of sales occur when somebody passes away. Often, the larger, more obviously valuable items are auctioned off, but the smaller things such as books, DVDs, minor jewelry, and so forth may be sold at low prices just to get rid of them.

For example, an estate might include drawer or several cigar boxes full of marbles, and on occasion, there may be large bottles or boxes filled with pounds of the little glass or clay spheres. The last thing anyone wants to do is figure out what each of these marbles is worth, even though some of them may have quite a bit of value. Often they will sell bottles or boxes full of them at a very low price.

Big-box stores such as Costco or Walmart are excellent sources of finding merchandise that's on sale or has a deep discount. You can purchase these and then resell them on EBay at quite a markup.

While I would never recommend that anybody shop during Black Friday, you can use those special days to get a few products that you can resell. Stay away from the obvious stuff like TVs and video game consoles, and search for markdowns on merchandise in the area of your expertise or passion.

Your neighbors and relatives may be good sources of things to sell. They probably have just as much clutter as you did before you started selling on EBay, and you could offer to help them declutter their belongings for a cut of the profit. Or you could just purchase their clutter in bulk. More than likely, they'll be happy to get rid of some old junk although you can be sure they'll be looking over your shoulder nervously as you go through their stuff.

Believe it or not, EBay itself is an excellent source of finding cheap merchandise to resell. When I first started, I put a boxed set of all of the James Bond movies on sale, and it got snapped up amazingly quickly. The buyer explained to me that he planned to resell the movies because they typically sell on EBay for about twice my asking price.

You can take advantage of Black Friday or Cyber Monday sales on Amazon and other similar sites and purchase products that have been steeply marked down, so much so that you can still make a good profit.

If your store becomes profitable enough, look for wholesalers who can provide products for you to sell on a regular basis. If you do this, get a sales tax ID so you can purchase the products without paying sales tax on them. Note you'll be expected to charge for sales tax on these items and pay that tax to the state.

The best way to find wholesalers, in my experience, is to ask other sellers where they get their products. Sometimes they will give up their source. You can even ask the local stores in your area for the names of their wholesalers.

Wholesalers often require that you purchase significant amounts of products from them on a regular basis. You typically can't buy one video or one doll; instead, you must purchase several cases of videos or a hundred toys, which you will then have to store in inventory somewhere until you sell them.

Drop shippers provide a service to ship products directly from their warehouse as you sell them on EBay. In this case, they store everything for you, maintaining inventories, and also do the shipping. Note they charge a fee for this service, and it's important to keep those in mind when you determine your pricing.

Just remember to stick to what you know, and expand into other types of merchandise slowly and cautiously to avoid being stuck with products that don't sell.

These are just a few examples of places that you can find merchandise in your local area or online. Keep your eyes open, and you'll find sources all over the place.

Listing Your Products

There are a lot of different things to consider when you're listing products for sale on EBay. You need to put them in the right category, include one or more pictures, write a great title and description, fill in as many specifics as you can, decide on a return policy and choose the shipping method.

EBay has several options to make this easier. I usually start by copying an existing listing for the same product. Be sure to review your listing carefully for accuracy, the title may include specifics that doesn't apply. When using this method, be wary for keywords in the title such as "new" when you are selling used products.

You can also define templates to use as a basis for your listings.

As you enter the information for your products, think about it from the buyer's point of view. If you were considering purchasing this product, what information would you need to make a decision?

Category — We've already gone over categories in the section Buying on EBay, but it's important enough discuss briefly once more. You must pick the right category for your product because it enables your buyers to find your merchandise. Be aware that selling products in improper categories is a violation of EBay terms and conditions and can cause the suspension of your account.

When you enter the product description, EBay attempts to find a category for you. I've noticed that it's pretty good at picking out exactly where the product needs to go, as long as a description is accurate.

Photos — See the chapter photos for a complete description how to enhance your listing with great pictures.

Title — Arguably, the title is the most important part of your EBay listing. The title is shown prominently in search results, and if it doesn't contain the right information, potential purchasers are going to move on to something else.

Additionally, EBay uses the title to group together similar items.

Your title needs to identify the product clearly and succinctly. For example, you could include the title of a book or movie, the type of product (marbles, Barbie dolls, fantasy miniatures), or other descriptive terms that tell both EBay and buyers about the merchandise.

You can also include some other keywords to help customers find your products. Look for examples of merchandise similar to yours and examine their titles. You are likely to find a few useful keywords or phrases.

Titles for books might include the author's last name and genre (science fiction, fantasy, mystery, romance and so forth.) Movies should include the title and perhaps the names of one or two of the actors, or the director.

When I was selling fantasy miniatures, I included the word fantasy miniature in my title, along with goblin, dragon, or some similar keyword.

It's also common to include the name of the manufacturer if you have room. Sometimes people search for equipment or supplies by the manufacturer.

Your space is limited so use it wisely. You don't need punctuation such as commas, periods, and semicolons. Separating each keyword by a space is sufficient.

Avoid using bizarre combinations of characters such as l@@k, save $$$$ and so on. These are equated to spam and turn off buyers.

Don't use filler words such as great, incredible, rare, old, wonderful, awesome and so on. These just take up space, don't help with indexing, and your average buyer filters them out mentally as they read the title.

Take the extra time to review the title, especially if you copied it from someone else's listing. When I first started selling movies, I copied listings for many of them. I didn't pay much attention until a purchaser pointed out that he received a used copy of a movie even though my title said it was new. I had accidentally carried over the word "new" when I copied the listing.

Inaccurate information can lead to unneeded refunds and negative feedback.

One thing you can do to increase your chances of being seen by the right buyer is to include a misspelling or two of your product name in the title. Take a look at the website *fatfingers.com* to see how this works on

EBay. For example, the brand Samsung is often mistyped as "samsunn". By including that word you might attract a few additional buyers.

Description — Take extra care to write an excellent description. Include all pertinent details about your product. Mention the type of product, title, condition, flaws, benefits, authors, actors, artists, and so forth.

Don't include a list of keywords or phrases, because this is a spamming technique known as keyword stuffing, and it may result in EBay removing the listing or even suspending your account. For example, "doll, dolls, porcelain doll, Barbie doll" is considered keyword stuffing. Don't include this kind of text in your description.

Think about it from the buyers the point of view. What would you want to know about the product?

Take a look at the descriptions that other people have written for the same or similar products. Feel free to borrow liberally, although you shouldn't just cut and paste. Write your description in your own words and don't plagiarize.

Factor in your profit to determine the amount of time you spend writing. For example, if you're selling a movie for $1.50, you might spend a lot less time then if you are selling a rare stamp for $1,000.

Take special care that the first couple of lines of your description carry the most weight. EBay uses these in their search algorithms. Do not, however, stuff those lines with keywords. That could cause EBay to mark your listing as spam, and may turn away buyers.

Check your grammar and spelling, because poor grammar and misspelled words will cost you lost sales. Keep your sentence length short and to the point.

Carefully documenting the condition of your product is vital. You must fully disclose anything non-optimal. I've sold old books — first editions — which were in fair condition. On one of them, the spine was cracked, there were some torn pages, and the dust jacket was missing. But because it was an older book and was collectible, I received a bid of several hundred dollars, and the buyer was very satisfied when he received it.

In another instance, I forgot to mention that the front cover had a very tiny dimple, about a quarter inch around. Other than that the hardcover was in perfect condition. The buyer complained, and I had to issue a refund and pay for a shipping label to get it returned to me. Fortunately, the client still gave me good feedback because of the quality of the communications and customer service that he received.

It is important to ensure that you describe the exact condition thoroughly in your description. Disclose every flaw, any scratches, writing, marks, dents or anything else that makes the item less-than-perfect. Doing this will prevent unnecessary refund requests and fraud reports to EBay.

Item specifics — To provide even more details about your product, you can specify item specifics. For example, the books category allows you to include the ISBN number and the type of cover: hardcover or paperback. On motorcycles, you can include the manufacturer's name and model number.

These specifics give buyers the opportunity to drill down to categories and subcategories of items that they want to find. By including item details, you make it more likely that customers will find your products.

Fill in as many details as makes sense for your product. Doing so will make it that much easier for buyers to find your merchandise make purchases.

Quantity — If you have more than one of the item to sell, specify how many when you define the listing. For example, I have about 20 copies of Writers of the Future Volume 31 for sale, so I show that in the listing.

WARNING: do not list the same item multiple times. Doing so violates EBay's terms and conditions, and they will suspend, and possibly even terminate your account. EBay runs automated processes which scan your listings to see if there are any duplicates.

Return policy — You have the option of whether or not to allow returns, and if you do, you can specify the length of time allowed. You can also ask the purchaser to pay for shipping the product back to you.

It's best to allow thirty days for refunds and returns. If a customer is dissatisfied, he's going to give you bad feedback, and that's going to affect future sales. If you allow unhappy customers to return and get refunds for products, then you improve your chances of getting better feedback.

Some products need to be sold "as-is", and in those cases specify no returns in the description. On a few old books that I've listed, I've specified no returns allowed, but thoroughly documented that the volumes had tears, broken spines, and so forth.

By taking the time to fill in all of the fields of the listing accurately and thoroughly, you improve the chances of making a sale and reduce the likelihood of getting a refund request.

Photos

Listings on EBay require at least one photo for each product, and you can include up to twelve without charge. Depending on the item, more and better pictures give your merchandise a greater chance of selling.

You can use your cell phone camera if you want — those can take relatively decent pictures — but a small, inexpensive digital camera works better because it can be placed on a tripod and has removable media, which makes it easier to transfer photos to your computer.

Get a lightbox or photograph on a light-colored blanket or something similar. Don't take pictures in the middle of your house, because customers want to focus on your product, not on the rest of your stuff.

Always include a nice clear shot of your product from the front. Use this as the first photo in the album, and make use of the cropping feature of EBay to clean up the images.

Include a shot from the side and back, and even the top and bottom if it makes sense. Sometimes placing a ruler behind the item helps to clarify its size.

It's important to include photos of anything about your product that is not optimal. Show all scratches, dents, dings, smudges, writing, frayed pages or any other damage of any kind in photographs.

Doing this will help prevent customers from purchasing your items and then claiming they didn't know about the problems and demanding a refund, leaving negative feedback and even reporting you to EBay.

Sometimes EBay will give you the opportunity to use a stock photo, which is a picture from their library, on new or like new items. You'll see this with books, movies and CDs. It's a good idea to use your own pictures rather than stock photos; I've found that customers tend to trust actual pictures of the products more than stock photos.

Sometimes when I've used stock pictures I've received emails from customers asking me to send them real photos because they didn't believe the stock photo represented my product.

The purpose of the photographs is to make your product look good and to build a level of trust between you and your buyers by showing any imperfections.

Again, you want to make your product looks enticing while at the same time clearly showing any flaws. Sometimes that can be a challenge, but it's worth the trouble because it will result in increased sales.

Auctions

An auction is a type of sale on EBay (as well as other similar sites) where buyers bid up the price of products, and the person with the highest bid at the end wins the purchase.

Auctions can be very lucrative if there is a high demand for your merchandise. Even if the bidding starts low, the price can go quite high depending on the quality of your listing and on the type of merchandise you are selling.

If you're reasonably confident the product will bid well, you can set the price low to lure in bargain hunters, and then watch it bid up higher and higher. There is some risk to the strategy because sometimes the price remains low and your product sells for less than you'd like.

To prevent that from being an issue, you can specify a reserve price, which is the minimum amount of money that you'll accept. Unfortunately, reserve prices tend to chase away bidders, because this means the lower bids don't count.

Thus, as a general rule, it's not a good idea to include a reserve price. If you believe there is a risk that the product will not bid up high enough to satisfy your requirements, then set the base price to the lowest value you'll accept.

Sometimes it's a good idea to set the initial price of your product at 99 cents. Before you do that, check out other similar products to ensure that the bidding was active, and they received a decent final bid. Otherwise, you might wind up shipping the product for far less than its worth.

The psychology of auctions is fascinating because often bidders get caught up in the excitement of the process. They keep bidding, even though the price has gotten quite high. It can be fun to watch this dynamic in action at an auction in the real world in addition to the virtual world of EBay.

For many items, auctions deliver a higher price than fixed-price listings. This applies in particular to collectibles, rare merchandise, and items that are in high demand or difficult to find elsewhere.

The most critical time for auctions is during their final hours. Smart bidders wait until the last minute to place a bid because this reduces the chance for counter offers. Inexperienced bidders — the vast majority — place bids at random times during the auction which merely drives up the price.

Listings that will expire soon are displayed higher in search results than those that have longer to run. For example, a listing which ends in 10 minutes will get shown before a listing which ends in an hour which gets displayed before any listings that end in 2 or 3 hours.

Time your auctions to the end in the evening — 10 PM EST works best because more people are at home and shopping. Sunday is the best day on which to end an auction while Friday and Saturday are the worst days.

In general, avoid the trap of ending an auction early at the request of a bidder trying to short-circuit the process. I have occasionally received a note from a potential bidder making an offer and asking me to end the auction prematurely. I have found it best just to tell them to join the bidding process take their chances.

Ending an auction on a holiday is a waste of time because many people are out doing other things rather than spending money on EBay.

If your bidder backs out of the sale, which has happened to me more than once, take advantage of EBay's second chance option to choose one of the other bidders to give them an opportunity to get the product at the price they bid.

Don't hesitate to experiment with your products and find the formats that work best for you and the items you're selling.

Fixed Price

Some products sell better as fixed-price rather than as an auction. Merchandise such as DVDs, ordinary books, CDs, and so forth seem to sell more quickly and at a higher price using the fixed-price format.

I've gotten the best results from fixed-price by including *Best Offer* on each listing. Most bidders accept my price for the merchandise without question, but a few will make an offer for a lower price. These are customers that you would otherwise lose, and it's an additional opportunity to make more income and sales.

For example, set the price of a movie at $5.95, then allow clients to make offers at a lower one. Nine times out of 10 the movie will sell at $5.95, but sometimes someone will request a lower price, perhaps $5.00 or so. I usually accept these because the price difference is so minor that it's better for me to move the merchandise than to hold out for a higher price.

Every once in a while, some customer will send an insanely low offer. In these cases, you can make a counter offer at a higher price. You can think of this as a negotiation between you and your client.

Let's say you list a movie at $5.95, and someone sends you an offer for $1.25. That's much too low of a price, so you counter offer for $4.95. Your client counter-offers for $3.00, and you make a final counter offer for $4.00, which your customer accepts. Note that EBay only allows two iterations of offers.

In my opinion, you should always include *Best Offer* because you'll sell more product faster, which is important. You can decline the offer, but some purchasers almost seem to make a game out of this and offer just a few pennies less than your price. I suppose it makes them feel like they got a bargain. By including *Best Offer*, you let them play their games while you still put money in your product.

As I mentioned with auctions, don't hesitate to experiment with the two different pricing formats. If it doesn't sell as fixed-price, then you can try relisting it as an auction the next time around. You may be surprised to find that it does better in the different format.

Pricing Your Product

The strategy of setting your price for auctions is different than for fixed-price sales. In fixed-price, set the price as high as you think will sell, while in an auction you typically set the price lower to get people to bid, hoping that it will go higher as the bidding proceeds.

Sometimes it doesn't matter what the merchandise has sold for the past or even what it is worth — you want to get a certain price, and that's just what you want. For example, I had a first edition, old book from 1951 which had a market value of between $500 and $600. I wasn't about to give it away for less than $1,000. For me, that's what it was worth. I put it on sale in an auction with a starting value of $1,000, and it sold for $1,200. Naturally, this strategy can backfire, and the merchandise may never sell at the price you set — but you can always change it later.

Fixed Price

Let's start with fixed-price, and the place to begin is to do a little bit of research. Put the name of your item in the search bar on EBay, then looked down the left side of your screen until you see the header *Show only*, and click *Sold listings, which* will show what the product has sold for the past.

Scan through the listings shown in this method finding those products that match yours to get an idea of the value.

You should also check out the same product with the *Sold listings* option unchecked to get a sense of the price for the current time.

If you don't have any idea what its worth, try searching for the product on Google to see if it is advertised online anywhere else.

Additionally, you can hire a professional to perform an appraisal of the product. For high dollar value merchandise, this can be of great benefit to prove to your buyers that your price is correct, and your product is as advertised.

Price also takes into account quality of your product. An unopened DVD in perfect condition will sell for a lot more than the same DVD that's been opened or damaged. There are exceptions to this rule. For example, sometimes used stamps — known as canceled stamps — sell for a lot more than those in mint condition. Your knowledge about what you are selling comes into play in these cases to help you decide on the right price.

Another variable is the price you paid, especially if you bought it specifically to sell on EBay. After all, you don't want to lose money if you can avoid it.

If you want to get rid of the product quickly, price it lower than the amount you found in your research. If the speed of the sale is not a concern, price it a little bit higher. Make a point to include the *Best Offer* option so that potential buyers who can't or won't meet your price have an opportunity to discuss it with you.

Auctions

For auctions, you define an initial price for the merchandise. People then place bids at progressively higher amounts. Each bid must be higher than the previous one.

For example, you list a product at 99 cents to begin with, which then receives an initial bid of $1.50. Throughout the week, the bids get higher and higher until the auction closes at a final price of $57.50.

You can start the bidding at any amount you want, but realize that higher opening values often result in a lower rate of bidding. Many people are looking for bargains and will avoid placing bids on higher-priced items.

You can get around that by putting a reserve amount on your merchandise. That allows you to set a very low opening bid, but your item will not sell unless it meets the reserve. This strategy is of limited value because many bidders stay away from merchandise with a reserve amount.

Shipping

Unless you're only selling items locally, which is usually not a good idea because it cuts out about 99% of your potential buyers, you will need to learn the ins and outs of shipping.

The completeness and accuracy of your listing are the first impressions that your client receives from you and your products. The speed and quality that you ship product are your next opportunities to make a good impression.

It is imperative to send your merchandise as soon as possible. Your best policy is to ship within a single day if you can. EBay automatically sends messages to customers when you print the postage and again when you ship the product.

To demonstrate how important this is, most of the comments in my feedback acknowledge that I ship quickly. The result of delays in shipping will be poor feedback and, more importantly, customers who are reluctant to return to your store.

The quality of your packaging is another opportunity to make a good, or bad, impression. Make sure your merchandise is well-padded and protected against damage.

Materials

When I began selling on EBay, the cost of shipping took me by surprise. It wasn't the postage that caused the reaction; I didn't anticipate the cost of the shipping materials. The price of boxes, tape, padding, envelopes and so on can eat into your profits, especially if you purchase them retail.

An office store sells boxes for anywhere from $1.50 all the way up to $10 or more, and padded envelopes can go for a buck each or even higher. A bag of Styrofoam peanuts sells for around $15, and a roll of bubble wrap is about the same price.

That kind of expense can reduce your profits, and if you are not careful, you may find yourself even losing money on some sales.

I searched around for better prices because I figured larger resellers are not paying those rates. With some research, I located all the supplies I needed on Amazon for far better prices.

A list of supplies is on this *page* on the Writing King website.

For example, my store is stocked with DVDs, CDs, and Blu-Rays. Amazon sells a box of fifty padded envelopes that are perfectly sized to ship these products. If I bought these at the local office store, I would pay about a dollar each; buying them in bulk from Amazon, I wind up paying around a quarter for each one.

Postage

EBay allows you charge for shipping in three different ways: the customer can pay the actual cost of postage, which doesn't cover materials; you can ask for a fixed amount for shipping, or you can offer free shipping.

If you choose to charge the actual cost, then the customer will pay for the postage only. When you select a calculated price for shipping, you may want to adjust your price up slightly to account for materials such as boxes, padding and shipping tape.

Setting the shipping charge too high drives away potential buyers, and could even violate EBay terms and conditions.

Don't use shipping as a profit center. The price that you charge for shipping should be your actual costs. Trying to pad your shipping to make a little extra profit chases away potential buyers.

I've run into products that had shipping charges of $40, $50 or even $75, which seemed excessive considering the products were domestic and relatively small and light. The seller had set a low price and was using the shipping charge to get a little bit more profit.

Products that are difficult to ship —framed prints with glass for example — require higher costs because they need special care, extra materials, and higher postage. Make sure you take this into account when you calculate your price.

You have the option of purchasing your postage direct from EBay or you can buy it yourself from your mail carrier.

Buying postage through EBay is a fantastic advantage for sellers. EBay has negotiated some excellent rates with the postal carriers, and they pass those discounts on to sellers. I have never had an instance where purchasing postage direct from the carrier saved money over EBay's charges.

I highly recommend getting shipping directly through EBay because it's both convenient and will save you money.

Types of shipping

You have the option to use different shipping companies, including the United States Postal Service and UPS. You can use whatever service provides you the best rate and service.

You also have your choice of box or envelope size and service offered by the shipping company. For instance, using the United States Postal Service you can ship via first class, priority mail, overnight and so forth.

If you're selling media such as books or magazines, media rate is virtually always the best option. The USPS offers a cut rate for shipping books, CDs, and movies.

Important note — magazines and comic books may not be shipped using media rate because they contain advertising. Media rate specifically excludes anything with advertising. It is irrelevant that the advertisements are years or even decades out of date. The USPS has the right to open media mail to validate you've followed the rules. If not, they will attempt to collect the unpaid postage from you.

For many of your products, USPS Priority mail is the best choice for shipping. The rates are good; the merchandise will receive priority service, and the Postal Service gives you boxes and envelopes at no charge. You can go to the USPS.com website to order supplies, and they will be delivered directly to your doorstep. Note that you cannot use these materials for anything except priority mail.

Free shipping

You can offer free shipping on your products, which means that you, the seller, pay for the cost of postage and shipping materials. Some dealers report this results in higher sales of their merchandise, but unless you're careful it can lead to reduced profits.

Personally, I haven't found that free shipping offers any real advantage, at least on the products that I've sold. The products don't seem to move any faster. Feel free to experiment and come to your own conclusions.

Combined shipping

Sometimes your customers will purchase several of your products at the same time. If you open an *EBay store*, this is even more likely to happen.

To give them an incentive to make multiple purchases, offer to combine shipping. By doing this, you ship all the products they ordered in one box or envelope instead of separately.

You get a break on postage because you're only paying for one package instead of many, so it is only fair to pass it on your customers. Not only do you save on the actual shipping charges, but you save money on materials and packing time.

EBay makes combining shipping easy because the shipping screen warns you that a single person has purchased multiple items, and asks if you want to merge them into one shipment.

The tracking code

If you buy your postage directly from EBay, you don't have to worry much about the tracking code. EBay will automatically assign the code for you and email that to both you and your purchaser. It's all automatic and straightforward.

If you purchase the postage yourself, be sure to enter the tracking code into EBay. They will send an email to message to the customer and assure them that the product is in the mail.

The only times I have not used EBay postage was when I shipped items that would fit in a regular-sized envelope, requiring only one or two stamps. In these cases, I didn't provide a tracking code.

International shipping

Shipping from the United States to other countries used to be a royal pain. The seller had to fill out customs documents and take care of all the details himself. It was so much effort that it was usually easier to skip allowing international sales.

With the advent of the Global Shipping Program from EBay, that has changed entirely. You ship your product to an EBay US address, and they take care of all the details such as customs documents, which makes it a no-brainer to allow for international shipping.

Check out the EBay help on international shipping for the rules and regulations.

Postal insurance

For most items, postal insurance is not necessary. In fact, it's usually an expensive option that doesn't give you any value. Most packages arrive at their destination in good condition, although I have found that heavier items tend to suffer damage more often than lighter merchandise.

As a rule, I purchase postal insurance only for merchandise worth several hundred dollars or more. It's certainly not necessary for smaller items like DVDs, CDs, and books.

Drop Shipping

Drop shipping is the practice of listing an item on EBay (or another site) that you don't have in your inventory. Instead, you list products which other web stores or drop shipping sites have in their inventory.

Let's say that a big box store like Walmart is running a great sale for a month on teddy bears. You know that teddy bears sell very well on EBay, so you create a listing for those products, but you don't actually purchase any teddy bears and don't maintain them in your inventory.

When you make a sale, you order the product from Walmart and ship it directly to your customer. You never have the actual product in your hands.

Drop shipping is great if you find products online at a steep discount. You have to be careful to note how long those price cuts last, because if they end while your EBay sale is active, you may lose money.

Drop shipping is allowed by EBay terms and conditions as long as the item delivery happens within thirty days after the end of your listing. Sellers are still responsible for the merchandise and buyer satisfaction just as if it was any other type of sale.

You don't have to inform your customer if you are using drop shipping, although, when they receive another company's box it will be pretty obvious.

Selling occasional drop-shipped products from online websites can work on a small scale, but it becomes awkward as quantities increase. A better option is to use an actual wholesaling drop shipping company such as *SaleHoo* or *worldwide brands*. Each of these companies requires a one-time fee to access their lists of thousands of wholesalers all over the United States or the world.

Drop shipping can be a great way to make a profit without actually putting out any money up front.

You have to be careful to choose items that sell because EBay will charge listing fees regardless of whether or not the merchandise the merchandise sold.

IMPORTANT NOTE: There are some scams which claim you can make a fortune by drop shipping using Amazon Prime to ship for free. These are SCAMS, and if you follow their advice, you will violate Amazon's terms and conditions and probably get your Amazon account suspended or terminated. Avoid any of the courses, books, websites, seminars or anything you see on the web about drop shipping. Instead, use one of EBay's Certified drop shippers.

You Made a Sale! What now?

Holy cow! You made a sale. Somebody bought something. Now, what?

Once EBay sends you an email saying the buyer has paid, your first objective is to ship the product as fast as possible. Customers enjoy receiving their merchandise quickly, and they get annoyed if it takes too long,

There have been many times when I've ordered things on EBay, and the seller didn't even bother to bring it to the post office for almost a week. That was annoying, and those sellers did not receive positive feedback from me. Like most buyers, I expect the seller to send the product quickly, within one or two business days at the most.

Carefully get your merchandise ready for shipping. Place smaller items in padded envelopes or small boxes. If the item is bendable, put a piece of cardboard on each side, which will not add much weight to your shipment, but it will help prevent damage.

Make a point to protect the corners of larger items. Use folded pieces of cardboard and shipping tape wrapped around each corner.

Using boxes and padded envelopes that are bigger than needed gives you room to include some padding materials to provide additional protection. Doing this is vital for larger, heavier products.

I sold a complete James Bond collection on DVD, which weighed several pounds, and found a nice snug box for shipping. By the time the buyer received this in the mail, four of the six corners had been damaged. I had to issue a refund and pay the shipping to get the product back to me. Since the collection suffered some damage, I had to sell it for about the third of its original value.

Use shipping tape to seal the box, and use more than is necessary. I always use extra shipping tape to ensure the box is going to stay sealed all the way to the buyer's location.

I recommend using EBay's built in shipping label application because it saves money — EBay gives you a discount off of shipping — and is extremely convenient. If you do this, you can print the labels directly from your computer to a printer and then tape them to the box or envelope.

Bring it over to the post office or your postal box, and ship them out.

If you use EBay's postal services, they will automatically send an email to your customer informing them of your shipment. This email contains the tracking code so the purchaser can get information on the progress of the delivery.

If you don't use EBay's built in postage service, enter the tracking code, if applicable, when you note the item as shipped. EBay will then send the same automatic message to the buyer.

As a caution, look for any instructions from the customer before you go to the trouble of boxing up the product and shipping it. I have found that special instructions are rare, and the one or two times I've missed them, I had to issue partial refunds.

In those cases, the special instructions requested shipping the product to a different address than the one listed on their PayPal account. By missing that instruction, I sent the product to the wrong address. To prevent negative feedback, I offered the buyers a partial refund of 25%, which they were happy to accept.

In most cases, this completes everything you need to do once you sell your products. You package it up, print and affix the postage, and drop it off at the post office.

Occasionally a buyer is dissatisfied. When this happens, prompt communication may prevent negative feedback. You might offer to issue a full or partial refund, and get the buyer to ship the product back to you if needed. For small items, I usually tell them to keep the product, since it will cost more to ship than it's worth.

Handling Refunds and Returns

There are many reasons for a dissatisfied customer. It could be a minor problem such as a scratch all the way up to the product never showing up at all.

In virtually all instances, it is a good practice to allow your buyers to return their product and receive a refund without question. Following this policy provides a high level of comfort and makes people more likely to make a purchase. Secondly, the buyer always has the option to enter negative feedback, and you can virtually always prevent that by refunding their money.

For most of the merchandise in my store, I allow the buyer to return the product for a refund for any reason. I do, however, ask them to pay for return shipping unless the problem is on my end, or there was damage in transit.

There are many reasons why someone may want a refund.

The product doesn't match the merchandise description on EBay – Sometimes the buyer will claim, rightly or not, that the product that he received does not match the description on EBay. Usually, this is a result of failing to disclose any flaws, no matter how tiny. Sometimes the problem could be as simple as listing the wrong edition of a book, not mentioning that a movie is widescreen, or even that there was a smudge on the cover.

For example, I listed a video game strategy manual as new because I'd never opened it and upon inspection I didn't see any flaws. However when the customer received the product, he noticed a slight dimple in the front cover. He demanded a refund and threatened to give negative feedback.

On another occasion, my listing stated in the title that the movie was a Blu-Ray. Unfortunately, I shipped a DVD instead, and when the customer received the product, he complained and left negative feedback. I offered a full refund, and the customer was happy to accept and changed the feedback to a positive comment.

When you create the listing for your merchandise, you can specify your return policy. Additionally, it is also good practice to write it out in the description of your item. It's best to be upfront and honest about your return policy.

Damaged in shipment — During transit, packages get dropped, thrown, cut open or suffer some other kind of harm. Buyers will always ask for a refund in these instances.

Damage is the responsibility of the seller, regardless of their return and refund policy.

The product never arrives — Sometimes the product never gets to where it's going. It just gets lost and never shows up at the destination. In this case, the seller is responsible for the loss and must refund the full amount.

The buyer didn't like it — There are times when the customer receives the product, and they just don't like what they received. Sometimes, to prevent negative feedback, you can offer a partial refund to resolve the situation.

Something strange is going on — I moved from California to Florida, and forgot to change the ZIP Code of my home office. One buyer figured that since my ZIP Code was close to their location, presumably California, they would receive the product more quickly. Once I shipped it, they realized that I was clear across the country, and it would take almost a week for the product to arrive. I received a scathing message explaining how much of an idiot I was for misrepresenting my location.

That's probably the strangest refund request I've ever received. I denied the request; thankfully the customer did not leave negative feedback.

Regardless of whether you allow returns or not, the buyer has the advantage in all of these transactions. They have the option to give negative feedback for any reason whatsoever.

To maintain an excellent record of feedback, in most cases it's best to accept the buyers reasoning, offer a partial or full refund, and if necessary ask them to ship the product back to you.

In these situations, excellent communication and negotiating skills come in handy. Enter into a dialogue with the dissatisfied buyer, find out what's on their mind, and make an offer to make amends for the problem, regardless of whether it's real or not.

There are occasions where I do not offer refunds on specific products which I have carefully photographed and listed any damage in the description.

I sold a first edition which was damaged. The pages were yellowed, the binding was frayed, and in a couple of places, the spine had separated. This was all carefully documented in the description and photographs. I noted that no refunds would be allowed on this item and that the photos recorded all flaws. Because of this documentation of the imperfections, the buyer was happy with what he received because he knew what he was getting.

You don't have to give them full refunds for the products. You can negotiate a partial refund in some cases.

I sold a game which was in a cardboard box, and the post office smashed one of the corners of the box in transit. The game was still playable, but it was damaged. I offered the buyer a 50% refund as long as they would not enter negative feedback, and they gladly accepted and left a very positive note.

Never threaten or badger a buyer. Always be honest, cheerful, and helpful to a fault. It's fine to negotiate as long as the negotiation is not a threat.

Remaining civil is an important point not only because it's just good business, but because the customer can report you to EBay if you threaten them or are hostile. EBay does not take this kind of behavior lightly.

In summary, it's best to offer thirty day period for returns and refunds. As long as you're honest in your description and pack your items well, you'll find that in general the refund and the return rate is very low.

In my experience, about one sale out of a hundred produces a refund request, and these are usually for something rational such as shipping damage or an incorrect description on the listing.

Allowing returns and refunds will help build confidence among your customers, and give them another reason to purchase from you. More importantly, it gives them a reason to come back to your *EBay store* for more purchases later.

Get them back with Good Customer Service

If you want to be successful as an EBay seller for the long-term, you must provide excellent customer service.

Begin customer service by creating good listings for your product. Include pictures that accurately show your products from various angles and any damage or deviations from the optimum condition. Your description should be accurate and to the point, and your refund policy should be spelled out.

Communicate with your customers as often as necessary. If you make a mistake, let them know. If they have a question, answer it right away. If you think of other products that they might enjoy, pop off a message with the information.

I accidentally shipped the wrong product to a customer. He ordered a video game, but I sent him a DVD instead. I just grabbed the wrong item and put it in the wrong envelope.

After I dropped the packages off the post office, got home, and saw the game sitting on the counter, I realized that I had made a mistake. I sent off an email to the client, even though it would be days before he knew there was a problem, admitted the error, and told him to keep the video with my compliments. I made it clear that I was shipping the game out to him that day and did so. He rewarded me with positive feedback and said he wouldn't hesitate to purchase from me again.

Whenever one of your customers sends you a message, answer it immediately and cheerfully. Ignore any emotion or anger in their message, and respond rationally and intelligently.

Customers will send questions to you on a regular basis. I get 3 to 4 messages a day asking the condition of this item, about combined shipping, or if I have something else they want. By answering promptly and nicely, I've turned many of these questions into sales.

If you specify *Best offers* on your merchandise, you'll receive a steady flow of messages from your customers offering a lower price for your products. For example, I listed a movie at $6.95 and received a *Best offer* for $4.95. I made a counter offer for $5.95, which the customer accepted. All of this occurred in a matter of a few minutes.

Ship your product quickly. Don't let the order set for more than a day if you can help it. If you want to create a business using EBay, instead of it just being a way to make a few extra bucks, then plan to ship product every working day of the week. Thus, the orders from today should be shipped tomorrow.

The quality of your shipping is also important. Poorly wrapped items get damaged easily in the mail, and they don't make a positive impression on your customers. Take the time to put your merchandise in a box in good condition or a padded envelope. If there's any danger of damage while shipping, especially to more expensive items, double box it (put the product in a small box inside a larger one) and use shipping peanuts for padding. The last thing you want to do is to issue a refund because of damage in shipping due to a poorly packed product.

It's a good idea to use EBay's internal email system to send messages. By doing this, all of your communication will be tracked by the EBay interface, and you can look them up later. Keeping these messages in the EBay system is handy if you have a dispute with a customer and need to prove your case. All of the email traffic between the two of you is at the fingertips of EBay support.

The key to good customer support is excellent communication. Communicate more than you think is necessary. They'll get the automatic message when they purchase the product, when it ships, and so forth. But it won't hurt to send additional messages as needed.

A thank you note can go a long way towards building repeat customers.

You can gain additional sales if you send a message pointing out other products that you sell that might be of interest to your buyer. For example, if you sell comic books, and they purchase a Spiderman issue, you could send them a link to the item in your EBay store with other Spiderman comics.

However, don't pester your purchasers with overly sales oriented messages. It's okay to send one or two now and then, but keep it to a minimum.

Remember, if you're on EBay for the long-term, the point is to build repeat customers, and not necessarily just to pull in another sale. By communicating and building those relationships, your clients will come back. Better yet, they may refer your EBay store to their friends, relatives, and acquaintances because they know you'll give them excellent service.

What about Feedback?

To hammer the point home, when you sell on EBay, one of your most valuable assets is your feedback score, which is an indication of how well you serviced your customers.

Each time you make a sale, your client has the option to leave feedback about the transaction. They are allowed to enter a score of good, neutral, or poor, and leave a comment explaining the reasoning. The idea is that before purchasing from a seller, you can check their feedback score and look at the comments, and get an indication as to whether they give good service, and their products are of high quality.

Note that the seller can also leave feedback for the buyer, which kind of evens things out a little bit. If the feedback comments show the buyer pays late, cancels bids, or returns items unnecessarily, a seller can reject the purchase.

Both of these scores are extremely useful for buyers and sellers. To be a prosperous EBay seller, it is vital that your feedback rating remains high, and the comments are positive.

Also, EBay gives added benefits, such as *top seller* and discounts, for those sellers who have high feedback scores.

It is interesting that the same score rates a person as both a buyer and a seller. Because of this, as explained earlier, a new seller can build up a better feedback score at the beginning by making some purchases and following through quickly with payment on every one of them.

Sellers need to go to extra lengths to make sure their feedback scores remain high, over 99% if possible. Personally, I tend not to purchase from EBay sellers who have it feedback score of less than 95%. To me, that indicates they have poor customer service, poor quality product, or some other issues.

I have found customers are almost always willing to give a good feedback score, or least neutral, if I have been honest with them, open about the issue, and make some attempt to resolve the problem.

For example, I shipped the wrong product to a customer accidentally. They received the product and sent an angry message back to me about the problem. If I shrugged my shoulders and left it at that, I would have received bad feedback. Instead, I immediately sent a message to the buyer, apologized for the problem, told them I would cover the shipping cost to send the product back, and immediately shipped the correct product at my expense (for shipping.) I received a very nice comment and a positive feedback score as a result.

On each and every problem that occurred, I've been able to negotiate a positive feedback score with the buyer. On a few occasions, when the product was relatively inexpensive, I told them to keep it and either refunded their money or sent them replacement product. At other times, I paid for return shipping and gave a partial refund for their inconvenience.

As long as you're doing a good job as a seller, problems such as these are few and far between. When you think about it, if you're making a couple of thousand dollars a month selling on EBay, and have to refund three $10 sales, you're doing pretty good.

Refund the money, pay for return shipping, and stay in good communication with your customers. That's virtually always the appropriate thing to do.

I'd like to caution you to ensure sure your attempts to negotiate through a negative experience remain upbeat and positive. Never threaten, never get emotional in a negative way, and never be angry with them. Keep your messages matter-of-fact and upbeat.

Never tell a buyer that if he gives you negative feedback you'll give him negative feedback. That's not a game you want to play. If you receive negative feedback, the best advice is simply to refrain from giving any feedback at all to your buyer.

Always apologize for any mistake, regardless of whether you believe it's valid or not. A quick "I apologize for the issue" is all that's needed.

Make sure you understand what the problem is, and if you don't, ask for more details or pictures.

One customer bought a pack of five CDs, but he made the assumption that it was a boxed set; I sent him five single CDs, virtually the same product, but he wanted the boxed set because he was giving it as a Mother's Day present. He received it the day before Mother's Day, so it was too late to send a replacement. I apologized and offered to split the difference, refunding half of the price of the product minus shipping and asked for a positive rating. He replied with a very nice email thanking me, accepted my offer, and rewarded me with a glowing feedback comment. Sure, I had to refund $7.50 to him, but it saved me from losing sales because of the negative feedback comment.

As I said at the beginning of this chapter, your feedback score is one of your most valuable assets. If you consistently give excellent customer service, sell quality products, describe them accurately in the description and photos, and work with any unhappy buyers, you'll be able to maintain a very high value.

It's worth the time and effort because a high score means that buyers are more likely to choose you over your competitors.

Relisting

It inevitably happens. You list a product on EBay, and it doesn't sell. You get a message in your email inbox telling you that you need to relist your product to give it another try.

Before you click that button, take a look at your listing.

Is the category correct? Perhaps you've got it listed in the wrong placc. Sometimes a minor change in placement can do the trick. For example, you might have placed a game in the category of "role-playing games" and perhaps "wargames" might describe the product more accurately.

Just keep in mind that your category should always be relevant to the product as it's a gross violation of EBay's terms and conditions to place merchandise incorrectly. That's considered spamming, and they will suspend or terminate your account if you do so.

How are the pictures? Do they accurately portray your product in a pleasant way which begs someone to purchase your products? Do you have enough photos? Are you using a stock photo?

If necessary, take new pictures or edit the existing ones. If you're using a stock photo, get rid of it and take your own pictures.

Is the title accurate and descriptive? Does it contain all the necessary keywords that people might use in their searches? Does it include useless words such as "incredible", "rare", and so on?

If needed, reword your description to make your product sound more attractive.

Look at everything else in your listing with a critical eye. Does it all make your product stand out? Does it make your product appealing? Does it accurately describe the product including any flaws?

Be sure to check out the price. Is it too high? Or even too low? Sometimes a price that is much too low can scare away buyers because it seems too good to be true – there must be something wrong with it.

After you've relisted the product several times, look at it with an even more critical eye. Is it something that other people want to buy? Is the quality so poor, as described in your description and photos, that you cannot get anyone interested? In these cases, your best option might be to drop the price low or to remove the product from EBay entirely.

Another option is to take some items that haven't sold and combine them into a lot of multiple products. For example, if you have ten movies that haven't sold in three listings, you might sell them all together as a single lot.

Finally, if the product simply doesn't sell, you might consider other options, and perhaps take it off sale for a time. Revisit selling the product at a later date. Another option is to sell it in a thrift store, at a yard sale, or even a flea market or swap meet.

For example, if your comic books haven't sold in three or four listings, then perhaps you should box them up and get a dealer to appraise them to see if they're worth anything at all. The dealer might purchase them for pennies on the dollar, or he might tell you that they are worthless.

The bottom line is to refrain from relisting your products blindly, especially after the second attempt. Analyze why they're not selling, and correct what is wrong. If they still don't sell, then come up with an alternative rather than bashing your head against the wall over and over. That will just cost you money and fees that will eat up your profits.

Watch out for the Fees!

Understanding EBay's fee structure is vital for you to make a profit. If uncontrolled, it's possible that these charges will not only reduce your income but even put you in negative territory.

The fees on EBay are easy to understand.

Insertion fee — This is the fee to create the listing. Each month, EBay allows you to create some listings without charge. The longer you've been selling, the more of these free listings you get. At the time of this writing, I'm paying twenty-five cents per listing after the free period. EBay charges the fee, unless it's one of the free ones, at the beginning of each month, regardless of whether or not the item sells.

Final value fee — This a percentage of the sale. You could call it EBay's "cut," which includes the price of the purchase plus any shipping and handling. EBay does not add Sales tax to this calculation.

Shipping charges — Shipping is not free. You can buy postage direct from EBay, or you can purchase it from a carrier of your choice. But shipping is always a cost (the only exception being if you list the item as *local pickup only*.) You have the option to charge the buyer for the shipping or to pay for it yourself.

Unless you add advanced listing options, that's all of the fees you need to worry about.

Advanced listing upgrades add options to make your listing stand out. These include bolding the title, including the listing in an extra-large gallery, listing in a second category, and so forth. These are optional, and you need to decide on a case-by-case basis whether or not the extra charges are worth the exposure.

You can see that if you're paying a quarter each time you list a video, and you're only selling it for a dollar, then after a few relists you may begin to lose money.

On a lower-priced item, say a foreign stamp which you are selling for a dollar, you might raise the price by the listing fee each time you relist. Otherwise, you may find yourself without any profit.

It's tempting to add the advanced listing upgrades, but they are seldom worth the money, and they heavily eat into your profit, especially on lower-priced items.

Remember to keep track of your fees and price accordingly, and you'll do just fine.

Set up an EBay store

Once you get beyond selling a few dozen items a month, it's time to set up an EBay store, which gives you a large number of advantages, and could potentially save you money.

It's beyond the scope of this book to get deeply into stores and all the options available. In fact, I could easily write another entire book (and probably will) just about how to set up one up and how to best use each and every option.

However, getting an EBay store is valuable, and should be discussed at least briefly.

There are several levels of stores, and each one has a different monthly fee. For most sellers, the lowest level store will work fine.

One immediate effect is listing fees become a lot cheaper, which saves you money as long as you sell enough products to offset the monthly charge.

I like the promotional tools included with stores. For example, you can create sales, which takes a percentage or a flat rate off the price of some of your items. The effect that a 10% off sale will have on your bottom line is amazing. People seem always to be looking for a bargain, and items on sale fit the bill for most of them.

For example, I listed several hundred DVDs for sale. About half of them sold the first time listed, so on the second listing, I placed the remaining half on sale for 10% off. A few weeks later, I changed it to 20% off, and then 30% off. By that time, most of the movies had sold, which is far better than sitting on a shelf.

You'll also gain the ability to create special promotions such as offering free shipping if more than a certain number of items are purchased, or even adding a free item for every fourth one bought. These promotions are often just the ticket for increasing profits.

I took advantage of this by offering free shipping with the purchase of five movies. Considering that shipping at media rate is $2.61 each item, that can save the buyer quite a bit of money. It's important that all five be shipped in the same box to reduce the total shipping charge.

The great thing about setting up an EBay store is you don't have to confront everything at once. There are hundreds of different options available. These include reports, tools to help you list items, options to create special promotions, email lists, flyers, and any number of other things.

You can try out each option one by one at your own pace.

To conclude, once you catch the EBay bug, and start selling product each month, paying the monthly fee for an EBay store makes sense. Once you do that, all of the various features available will allow you to increase your sales and most likely result in much higher profits.

Promoting your Store

Creating a store gives you access to quite a few tools. These allow you to create sales, print a flyer, send out an email newsletter, and create various promotions.

Markdown Manager — This handy tool lets you select one or more items from your store and put them on sale. You can subtract a fixed amount or percentage. On your listing, the old price will be crossed out and the sale price shown to make it obvious that the prices have been marked down.

Promotional Flyer — You can increase your follow-on sales from your customers by using the promotional flyer, which allows you to print a sheet of a few items from your store. You can include this in the boxes and envelopes that you ship to your clients.

Email Marketing — Customers can subscribe to your EBay email newsletter, which will list various products from your store. This newsletter is useful for keeping customers who like your store informed of products they might enjoy.

Promotions — EBay has some very nice features to offer regarding promotions. Using the tool in your store, you can create a digital coupon, specify free shipping or a free product if a certain amount of item are purchased, and put a discount on items based on conditions. It's a great way to get customers to add a few more of your products to their shopping cart.

You can also promote your store outside of EBay, which are familiar to anyone who has done Internet marketing.

While Facebook is not a sales tool, per se, you can on occasion post a link to your store or a particular product or category you want to promote. Be sparing with this, as it tends to cause friends to unfollow or unfriend you if done too often.

Include the web address of your EBay store in the profiles of all of your social media accounts. That way anybody who's checking you out can also check out your store.

The web address of your store should be included in your email signature, printed on your letterhead, and included anywhere else visible.

Don't forget about your website, your blog, and so forth. If you have a presence on the web, by all means use it to promote your store. Include the link in your about page, and in the footers of every page on your blog or website.

You can set up your own storefront website and use it to promote your EBay products. Doing this gives you more control over how to display the products and provides another method for search engines and people to find your store.

Rewarding Good Sellers

EBay rewards sellers who consistently give good service, resolve issues with buyers quickly and efficiently, don't violate EBay terms and conditions, and consistently sell merchandise.

When you first begin selling on EBay, you will be restricted to only listing a certain dollar amount and number of listings. Month by month, as you perform well, EBay will raise these limit so you can sell more and make more money.

The concept is to require sellers to confirm information with EBay and to prove that they can sell efficiently and follow the rules.

EBay is very sensitive to poor feedback, and a high quantity of negative comments and ratings may result in higher fees and other penalties.

Handle any refund requests quickly. Don't argue, just give them their money back (full or partial as the situation demands.) Never allow any transaction to escalate to *EBay's Money Back Guarantee* or *PayPal Purchase Protection*. These programs act as insurance to protect buyers against sellers who are scammers or disreputable.

I think its obvious sellers should be selling merchandise on EBay. The lack of selling will prevent you from getting the limits removed and raising to *Top Seller* and *Power Seller* status. By the fact that you've created a seller account, EBay has an expectation that you intend to sell.

Become familiar with EBay's terms and conditions and policies, and follow them consistently.

Make sure you aren't selling anything illegal, unauthorized, or counterfeit. Never sell bootlegged or pirated copies of anything, which EBay frowns on because it violates the legal copyrights of the rightful owners.

If you consistently meet the above guidelines for several months, EBay will raise your selling limits — both the quantity and dollar amount.

You can call EBay's customer service to request higher limits, and they're good about granting them if you've proven yourself to be a consistent and ethical seller.

Top Rated Seller

If you consistently meet EBay's performance standards for selling product and tracking your shipments, you can qualify to become a *Top Rated Seller*.

When this happens, EBay adds an icon which is displayed next to your name on your listings in your store and gives you 20% discount on final value fees.

Top Rated Plus

Once you're a *Top Rated Seller*, you can easily qualify to be a *Top Rated Plus* seller by providing a thirty-day return policy and shipping within a business day of purchase. EBay adds a seal or icon to the display of your items to show buyers that you provide top service.

Power Seller

You can qualify for *Power Seller* status if you continue to sell products at a good rate on EBay, keep your account in good standing, maintain a positive feedback of 98% or higher, follow all policies, handle returns and refunds quickly and efficiently, and sell at least one hundred transactions worth $3,000 in a year.

Depending on the dollar amount of your sales, you can go up levels of *Power Seller* including Bronze, Silver, Gold, Platinum, and Titanium.

Being a power seller gives you customer service phone support from 6 AM to 10 PM Pacific time and some other benefits that can save you money and help you improve service to customers.

Moving to these levels means that you are performing well as an EBay seller. EBay rewards consistent sales and excellent customer service with discounts and added features.

More importantly, moving up entices people to buy from you over and over again.

It's a great reward system, and I find that it works very well. EBay encourages me to be responsible, to sell products, and to follow the rules.

Running Afoul of EBay's Rules

Like everything else, EBay has rules. These are described in their terms and conditions, and in various places in their tutorials and help system.

One of the first things you should do when you start to sell on EBay is review those rules and become very familiar with them.

It's important to understand your responsibilities, your rights, and those things that are forbidden. There are too many of these to list here entirely, but I'll give you a few examples.

On occasion, I receive an email from a buyer requesting that they pay outside of EBay "to save shipping costs and fees." Doing this is strictly forbidden by EBay policy, and representatives have told me this practice can cause the termination of an account. If you don't want to pay EBay's fees, then don't sell your products or EBay. It's that simple.

When I was first beginning, I accidentally entered a movie twice as two separate listings. An automatic application runs on EBay every once in a while to look for duplicate listings because that's a common spamming technique. If it finds duplicates, EBay suspends your ability to add more listings for seven days.

After this had happened to me, I talked at length with the EBay representative (EBay's customer support group is outstanding) and learned a lot about what a seller can and can't do.

One thing EBay will not do is lift that kind of suspension. At least in the case of duplicate listings, if caught, you cannot add listings for seven days, and there is no appeal. I suspect this penalty gets worse on future occurrences, but I have no intention of ever allowing it happen again.

You should never try to make a little extra money by overcharging for shipping. I've seen a lot of listings that have extremely high shipping charges, and that's frowned upon by EBay. If they catch you, which will happen if the customer opens a complaint, I'm sure there will be repercussions. I make it a point to charge the actual cost of shipping, so I don't need to worry about this.

In the course of our discussion about duplicate entries, the EBay representative let me know that putting an item in the wrong category is also something that could get your account suspended. She told me this is a technique often used for spamming.

Your EBay listing should never link to outside websites. Just don't do it at all.

Keyword stuffing and other spamming techniques are highly frowned upon, and you should refrain from using them. Just make your listings as descriptive as possible without trying to scam the system.

If you do get caught doing something that falls outside of EBay's policies, keep your cool and remain calm and friendly. Ask what you did wrong, why it violates the policies, and how you can keep from doing it in the future. EBay may or may not lift the penalty, but you're going to get a lot more traction if you don't get angry or upset with them.

The best policy is to understand EBay's terms and conditions and policies, then follow them to the letter. You can't go wrong if you do that.

Conclusion

EBay is, in my mind, by far the best merchandise selling platform on the Internet. They have all of the tools necessary to provide a favorable environment for both buyers and sellers.

If you have things to sell, perhaps the clutter in your home, then EBay is a great place to make a few extra dollars. If you're like me, it won't be long before you catch the "EBay bug" and start making some real income by selling things on the web.

A great place to begin selling is to de-clutter your belongings. Virtually everyone owns things that they no longer use or no longer need. Books they've read and will never read again. Movies they will never watch. Toys from children who have grown up and left the house. Games that have sat on the shelf for years or old video game consoles collecting dust.

Equipment such as old computers, tablets, cell phones and smartphones, disk drives, and accessories are great items to sell on EBay.

If you have a storage unit or closet or two that is full of things that you haven't even looked at in years, then certainly consider using EBay to make some extra money from stuff you already own.

There is no upfront cost to selling on EBay. You pay your fees when you sell. You don't have to purchase anything at all to list a few products for sale unless you decide to pull them off sale later. In that case, you will owe EBay the listing fees.

The best advice is to purchase a few things to become familiar with EBay and how it works, and then just jump in and start selling. Begin with smaller things that are easier to sell to get used to the interface and build up your feedback scores.

Most of all have fun, understand the rules and regulations and follow them, and don't take it too seriously.

Over time, you may decide to make real money and expand into drop shipping or finding local sources for products that you can resell.

Good luck, and learn how to use EBay to the fullest to supplement your income. You might be surprised at how much you earn.

Before you go

If you scroll to the last page in this eBook, you will have the opportunity to leave feedback and share the book with Before You Go. I'd be grateful if you turned to the last page and shared the book.

Also, if you have time, please *leave a review on Amazon*. Positive reviews are incredibly useful. If you didn't like the book, please email me at *rich@thewritingking.com* and I'd be happy to get your input.

linkedin.thewritingking.com

About the Author

https://www.linkedin.com/in/richardlowejr

Richard Lowe has leveraged more than 35 years of experience as a senior computer manager and designer at four companies into that of an author, blogger, ghostwriter, and public speaker. He has written hundreds of articles for blogs and ghostwritten more than a dozen books. He's published factual books about computers, the Internet, surviving disasters, management, and human rights. He's currently working on a ten-volume science fiction series, to be published at the rate of three volumes per year, beginning in 2016.

Richard started in the field of Information Technology, first as the Vice President of Consulting at Software Techniques, Inc. Because he craved action, after six years he moved on to work for two companies at the same time: he was a Vice President at Beck Computer Systems and the Senior Designer at BIF Accutel. In January 1994, Richard found a home at Trader Joe's as the Director of Technical Services and Computer Operations. He remained with that wonderful company for almost 20 years before taking an early retirement to begin a new life as a professional writer. He is currently the CEO of The Writing King, a company that provides all forms of writing services, and a Senior Branding Consultant for *LinkedIn Makeover*.

Richard has a quirky sense of humor and has found that life is full of joy and wonder. As he puts it, "This little ball of rock, mud, and water we call Earth is an incredible place, with many secrets to discover. Beings fill our corner of the universe, and some are happy, and others are sad, but each has their unique story to tell."

His philosophy is to take life with a light heart, and he approaches each day as a new source of happiness. Evil is ignored, discarded, or defeated; good is helped, enriched, and fulfilled.

Richard spent many happy days hiking in national parks, crawling over boulders, and peering at Indian pictographs. He toured the Channel Islands off Santa Barbara and stared in fascination at wasps building their homes in Anza-Borrego. One of his joys is photography, and he has photographed more than

1,200 belly dancing events, as well as dozens of Renaissance fairs all over the country.

Because writing is his passion, Richard remains incredibly creative and prolific; each day he completes between 5,000 and 10,000 words, diligently using language to bring life to the world so that others may learn and be entertained.

Richard is the CEO of The Writing King, which specializes in fulfilling any writing need. You can find out more at *http://www.thewritingking.com*, and emails are welcome at *rich@thewritingking.com*

Books by Richard G Lowe Jr.

Business Professional Series

Over 100 Tips to Improve Your Professional Life: Professional Ethics - have you ever wondered what it takes to be successful in the professional world? This book gives you some tips that will improve your job and your career.

Help! My Boss is Whacko!: Tips to help you deal with unprofessional behavior from the boss - sometimes the problem is the boss. There are all kinds of managers, some competent, some incompetent, and others just plain whacked. This book will help you understand and handle those different types of managers.

Help! I've Lost My Job: Tips on What to do When You're Unexpectedly Unemployed – suddenly having to leave your job can be a tough and emotional time in your life. Learn some of the things that you need to consider and handle if this happens to you.

Help! My Job Sucks Insider Tips on Making Your Job More Satisfying and Improving Your Career – sometimes conditions conspire to make the regular trek to a job feel like a trip through Dante's Inferno. Sometimes, these are out of our control, such as a malicious manager or incompetent colleague. On the other hand, we can take control of our lives and workplace and improve our situation. Get this book to learn what you can do when your job sucks.

How to Manage a Consulting Project: Make money, get your project done on time, and get referred again and again – I found that being a consultant is a great way to earn a living. Managing a consulting project can be a challenge. This book contains some tips to help you so you can deliver a better product or service to your customers.

Insider Secrets for Managers and Supervisors: Lessons Learned Managing from the Trenches – I've been a manager for over thirty years I learned many things about how to get the job done and deliver quality service. The information in this book will help you manage your projects to a high level of quality.

<u>Computer Safety Series</u>

Safe Computing is Like Safe Sex: You have to practice it to avoid infection – Security expert and Computer Executive, Richard Lowe, presents the simple steps you can take to protect your computer, photos and information from evil doers and viruses. Using easy-to-understand examples and simple explanations, Lowe explains why hackers want your system, what they do with your information, and what you can do to keep them at bay. Lowe answers the question: how to you keep yourself say in the wild west of the internet.

<u>Disaster Preparation and Survival Series</u>

Real World Survival Tips and Survival Guide: Preparing for and Surviving Disasters with Survival Skills – CERT (Civilian Emergency Response Team) trained and Disaster Recovery Specialist, Richard Lowe, lays out how to make you, your family, and your friends ready for any disaster, large or small. Based upon specialized training, interviews with experts and personal experience, Lowe answers the big question: what is the secret to improving the odds of survival even after a big disaster?

Creating a Bug Out Bag to Save Your Life: What you need to pack for emergency evacuations - When you are ordered to evacuate—or leave of your free will— you probably won't have a lot of time to gather your belongings and the things you'll need. You may have just a few minutes to get out of your home. The best preparation for evacuation is to create what is called a bug out bag. These are also known as go-bags, as in, "grab it and go!"

Professional Writer Series

Freelance Writing Business - Insider Secrets from a Professional Ghostwriter: Proven Tips and Tricks Every Author needs to know about Freelance Writing – This book explains how to be a ghostwriter, and gives tips on everything from finding customers to creating a statement of work to delivering your final product.

How to Write a Blog Post that Sells: Proven Tips and Tricks Every Blogger Needs to Know – There is an art to writing an article that prompts the reader to make a decision to do something. That's the narrow focus of this book. You will learn how to create an article that gets a reader interested, entices them, informs them, and causes them to make a decision when they reach the end.

<u>Other Books by Richard Lowe Jr</u>

How to Surround Yourself with Beautiful Women: Without Being a Sleazeball – I am a photographer and frequently find myself surrounded by some of the most beautiful women in the world. This book explains how men can attract women and keep them as friends, which can often lead to real, fulfilling relationships.

Expert Tips on Throwing a Party and Socializing: How Every Person Can Succeed with Putting On A Party Event – Many of us have put on parties, and I know it can be a daunting and confusing experience. In this book, I share what I learned from hosting small house parties to shows and events.

Additional Resources

Is your career important to you? Find out how to move your career in any direction you desire, improve your long-term livelihood, and be prepared for any eventuality. Visit the page below to sign up to receive valuable tips via email, and to get a free checklist for keeping your career on track and going strong.

http://list.thewritingking.com/

I've written and published many books on a variety of subjects. They are all listed on the following page.

https://www.thewritingking.com/books/

On that site, I also publish articles about business, writing and other subjects. You can visit by clicking the following link:

https://www.thewritingking.com

To find out more about me or my photography, you can visit these sites:

Personal website: *https://www.richardlowe.com*
Photography: *http://www.richardlowejr.com*
LinkedIn Profile:
https://www.linkedin.com/in/richardlowejr

If you have any comments about this book, feel free to email me at *rich@thewritingking.com*

Recommended Products and Services

LinkedIn Makeover

It's a tough job market out there, and many people are struggling to find jobs. A big part of the job search process is LinkedIn. In fact, it's been stated that 80% of employers today use LinkedIn to find prospective employees.

Having a strong LinkedIn profile that speaks to your abilities and sells you as the perfect job candidate is paramount.

That's where Donna comes in! She helps you craft a professional, bright and POWERFUL LinkedIn profile, so you stand out from the crowd and intersect with more opportunities. *Check her out.*

http://makeover.thewritingking.com

Other Products

For a list of all other recommended products, please visit this page:

https://www.thewritingking.com/recommended-products/